WORKING MY WAY BACK

A GUIDE FOR EX-OFFENDERS SEEKING EMPLOYMENT

MAURICE HAMILTON

HAYMAKER PUBLISHING
CHARLOTTE, NORTH CAROLINA

WORKING MY WAY BACK

Library of Congress Number: 2011936685
International Standard Book Number: 978-0-9839278-0-8

My heartfelt thanks go out to the cadre of persons who have given me their love, support, counsel, challenge, and even doubts. Each one of you has enlightened me in some small way.

This book is dedicated to my wife, my children, and to all ex-offenders looking for jobs and making every effort to change their lives for the better. *I must extend a special thanks and acknowledgment to editors at Creative Space.*

"Even if you're on the right track,
you'll get run over if you just sit there."

– *Will Rogers*

CONTENTS

"Change has a considerable psychological impact on the human mind. To the fearful it is threatening because it means that things may get worse. To the hopeful it is encouraging because things may get better. To the confident it is inspiring because the challenge exists to make things better."

– *King Whitney Jr.*

INTRODUCTION

This booklet is designed to prepare ex-offenders for employment. If you follow the instructions carefully, they will greatly improve your chances of getting a job. Many ex-offenders become repeat offenders because once they are released back into society with a prison record, they can't land a job.

The first thing to remember is this: **You can do it!**

Forget about your past, and forget about the crime you committed, because you have paid your debt, accepted your punishment, and served your time. Keep that in mind every day, and others will see that you're ready to move on!

You will get back on track if you are willing to do what it takes. In most cases, it's going to take more than passion and enthusiasm. It will probably require going back to school. It's often said that knowledge is power, and it's true. Having the right skills and knowledge will make the difference and prepare you for that opportunity.

According to the U. S. Census Bureau, a person without a high school diploma will earn an average of $400 a week. Those with a bachelor's degree earn an average of $900 a week.

The opportunity will come. Are you ready?

Let's get started!

"Success in business requires training and discipline and hard work. But if you're not frightened by these things, the opportunities are just as great today as they ever were."

– *David Rockefeller*

OPPORTUNITIES AND WHAT TO EXPECT

The Goodwill Connection

Goodwill industry has a 109-year history of helping people find jobs. Some of the services you may access through Goodwill include the following.

Pre-release services. If you are still incarcerated, get a head start on building your work skills and obtaining the necessary documentation to start your job search *before* you are released. Talk to the prison administrator, prison advisor, parole officer, a minister, or all of the above. Let people know that you are ready to redeem yourself and become a productive and contributing member of society. Ask them to be your mentor as you prepare for life on the outside.

Basic skill development. Earn your high school diploma or GED by taking basic education classes. Many prisons offer these courses. If yours does not and you live in New York, contact the New York State Education Department:

Patricia M. Mooney, GED Administrator
New York State Education Department
89 Washington Avenue, Room 306 EB
Albany, NY 12234
Public Hotline: (518) 474-5906
State Administrator: (518) 486-2182
Fax: (518) 486-5746

If you live in a different state, check with your state or city's education department to find out which programs they offer.

Employment readiness training.
Learn "soft skills"—how to interview and how to communicate in the workplace—that will help you succeed at work.

Occupational training.
Learn a trade. Becoming a machinist, bricklayer, or chef can get you back to work.

Life skills.
Check a book out of the library, and learn new skills that help you round out your life: parenting, relationship, and communication skills. Every library has an information desk that will help you find what you need.

Find someone with the skills to teach you how to write your resume and cover letter. Find mentors who can teach you how to sell yourself and negotiate an offer. [1]

Job placement assistance:
These skills and the help of Goodwill employment specialists will open doors to employment opportunities. Be sure

to contact your local Equal Employment center or the State Department of Labor training programs. They offer free training to the unemployed for trades that the local community may need such as maintenance, construction, and restaurant work.

"Man often becomes what he believes himself to be. If I keep on saying to myself that I cannot do a certain thing, it is possible that I may end by really becoming incapable of doing it. On the contrary, if I have the belief that I can do it, I shall surely acquire the capacity to do it even if I may not have it at the beginning."

– *Mahatma Gandhi*

You CAN do it!

SAMPLE JOB APPLICATION

In addition to submitting a resume, many potential employers will require you to complete a job application. This way they will have consistent data on file for all prospective applicants. Also, your signature on the job application acknowledges that the information is accurate. Below is a sample application:

Business name
Business address
Telephone number
Fax number
Email address

Name: ____
Present address: _____________________________________
Permanent address: ___________________________________
Email address: _______________________________________
Home phone: ___________ Work phone:______________
Social Security number: ______________________________
Person to contact in case of an emergency:
____
Phone: ____
Date of birth:____
Height: __________________ Weight: _________________
Marital status: ___________ Maiden name: ____________
Driver's license number: ______________________________

Job objective: ______________________________

Date you can start: ______________________________

Desired salary: ______________________________

Other job interest: ______________________________

Willing to locate? ______________________________

Area preference: ______________________________

Education:

Highest school grade completed: ____________________

Do you have a high school diploma? ________________

Name and location of education institution:

____

Degrees received Major/specialty Dates attended

___________ ______ ______ ______________

___________ ______ ______ ______________

___________ ______ ______ ______________

Other classes (including conferences, workshops, seminars):

____

____

____

____

____

Honors, achievements, extracurricular activities, hobbies, or interests:

____

____

____

____

Employment record (In reverse chronological order)

Dates of employment: ____________________________

Name of organization: ______________________________
Address: ______________________________
Title or position: ______________________________
Duties: ______________________________

Name of supervisor: ______________________________
Reason for leaving: ______________________________
____
____
____
____
____
____
____

Professional, union, social memberships: ______________
____

Military service ______________________________
Branch of service: ______________________________
Date of entrance: ______________________________
Date of discharge: ______________________________
Military assignments/Occupational specialty: ____________
____

Explain any special circumstances: __________________
____

Prior convictions: ______________________________
Have you ever been convicted of any violation of law, including moving traffic violations? ____________________
If yes, please provide the following:
Describe the offence: ______________________________
In which city, county, and state the incident occur?
____

Date of charges: ________________________________

Date of conviction: ______________________________

Explain any personal responsibilities or health problems that might prevent you from coming to work such as defects in hearing, vision, or speech.

____

____

____

Work start date: When will you be available to start work? Month: _____ Day: ______ Year: _______

Job application certification:

I hereby certify that all entries on this application and any attachments are true and complete. I also agree and understand that any falsification of this information may result in my forfeiture of employment.

Applicant's signature: _____________________________

Complete all the questions, and be honest with your answers. You don't want to get a job and lose it because you gave false information on your application. Misrepresenting yourself at any stage of the hiring process can cost you a job opportunity.

WHAT IS A COVER LETTER?

A cover letter is a letter of introduction that should be attached to another document such as a resume. Employers may use a cover letter as one method of screening out applicants who do not demonstrate sufficient interest in the position or who lack job hunting or writing skills.

Cover letters should be no longer than one page and divided into a header, introduction, body, and closing.

Header.
Cover letters use standard business letter style, with the sender's address and other information, the recipient's contact information, and the date sent after either the sender's or the recipient's address. The final part of the header is a salutation (e.g., "Dear Mr. Simms").

Introduction.
The introduction briefly states the specific position you desire and should be designed to catch the employer's immediate interest.

Body.
The body highlights or amplifies on material in the resume or job application, and explains why you are interested in

the job and would be of value to the employer. Matters discussed typically include skills, qualifications, and past experience. If there are any special issues to note such as your availability date, they may be included here as well.

Closing.

A closing sums up the letter and indicates the next step you expect to take. You may simply say that you look forward to hearing from or speaking with the employer. After the closing, include a valediction ("Sincerely") and your signature. Optionally, the abbreviation "ENCL" may be used to indicate that there are enclosures. [2]

SAMPLE COVER LETTER

August 15, 2020

Attention: Darren Simms
Business Name
Business Address
City, State ZIP

Dear Mr. Simms,

I would like to apply for the engine repair technician position that you have listed with the Mecklenburg County Employment Services in Charlotte, North Carolina.

As you will see by my attached resume, I have experience doing engine repair, drivability/engine performance, electrical/electronic systems, and automatic transmissions/transaxles.

In my personal time, I attended a training program at Central Piedmont Community College, Charlotte, North Carolina. This course helped me to become educated about engine principles and engine electrical systems analysis.

I can be reached at 000-111-2222 to schedule an interview. I hope to hear from you to discuss this exciting opportunity with your company.

Sincerely,

Your name
Your mailing address
City, State ZIP

ENCL: Resume

WHAT IS A RESUME?

A resume is a one- or two-page summary of your skills, experience, and education. While a resume is brief and concise, it highlights your accomplishments to show a potential employer that you are qualified for the work you want. It is not a biography of everything you have done.

Its purpose is to get you an interview.

A resume can (and often should) reflect more than just your paid work experience. Current students, in particular, should consider including the details of more important extracurricular, volunteer, and leadership experiences.

If you have worked in more than one career, it might be appropriate to have separate resumes to fit each field.

You can find and attend a resume workshop or have your resume reviewed at a Career Center or by your Career Advisor. [3]

SAMPLE RESUME

John Doe
123 Main Street, Charlotte, NC 28234
Phone (555) 555-5555 • Email name@email.com
GENERAL MOTORS CERTIFIED/MASTER CERTIFIED TECHNICIAN
Offering 6 years of Cadillac Specialization Experience

I am a Well-qualified ASE Master and General Motors (GM) technician with six years of experience in a fast-paced, high-volume dealership. I have an associate degree in GM Automotive, extensive Cadillac drivability, electrical, and transmission experience. I am motivated, hardworking, reliable, and productive with a proven ability to deliver high-quality work and excellent customer satisfaction. Areas of strength include the following:

- Drivability/engine performance
- Manual drive train and axels
- Engine repair
- Heating/air conditioning
- Electrical/electronic systems
- Brake systems
- Automatic transmission/transaxle
- Suspension and steering

Qualification Highlights

Produce an average of 60 flat-rate hours weekly performing GM diagnostic analyses, repair, and maintenance work as the only technician on the dealership's GM team experienced with Cadillac drivability, automatic transmission/transaxle, and diesel.

Maintain an excellent customer satisfaction rate with virtually zero comebacks. Interface professionally and communicate easily with customers, service writers, and coworkers. I am known for integrity and honesty in all customer dealings.

Upsell 20+ hours each month, accurately assess problems and needs, and provide adequate information and advice for customer decision making.

Trained and certified in all GM and Cadillac-specific courses. Maintain up-to-date, working knowledge of all new scan tools and GM.

Knowledgeable in computer systems such as SI2000, Tech Link Online, and Tech II.

Achieved ASE Master Technician certification, EPA certified, A/C Qualified Technician. Scanning and licensing as a North Carolina state-certified inspector.

Assist service manager and writers by locating required bulletins and warranty information and responding to customer telephone inquiries on technical problems.

Work History

General Motors Technician
Memorex Motors (Cadillac, Pontiac, Chevy, and Nissan dealers), Charlotte, NC 2000–2011

Automotive Center Associate
Sears Auto Center, Matthews, NC 1997–2000

Assistant Automotive Technician
Robert's Complete Auto Repair, Detroit, MI 1993–1997

Education

AS General Motors Automotive with Dean's List Honors
Motor City Technical College—Detroit, MI 1996

Certified in all GM/Cadillac courses, GM Training Center, Detroit, MI 1993–1997

Awarded "Best Student" and graduated with honors from two-year high school auto and shop program

References available upon request

AGENCIES THAT HELP THE UNEMPLOYED OR EX-OFFENDERS

The following agencies provide services that can help you to locate job training programs and jobs.

Office of Correctional Job Training and Placement

320 First Street NW
Washington, DC 20534
Telephone: (800) 995-6423 Ext. 147 or
(202) 307-3361 Ext. 147
Website: http://www.bop.gov/nicpg/nicmain.html

State Department of Labor

The toll-free help line provides a full range of basic information about workforce program services for workers and employers. Information is available in over 140 languages. Call 1-877-US2-JOBS (TTY 1-877-889-5627) or visit their website: www.dol.gov

The Correctional Education Association

4380 Forbes Boulevard
Lanham, MD 20706
Telephone: (301) 918-1915
Fax: (301) 918-1846
Website: http://sunsite.unc.edu/icea/

The Office of Correctional Education

600 Independence Avenue SW, MES 4529
Washington, DC 20202-7242
Telephone: (202) 205-5621
Fax: (202) 401-2615
Website: http://www.ed.gov

The National Institute of Corrections

1860 Industrial Circle, Suite A
Longmont, CO 80501
Telephone: (800) 877-1461
Fax: (303) 682-0558
Website: http://www.bop.gov/nicpg/nicinfo.html

United Way of Central Carolinas, Inc.

301 S Brevard St
Charlotte, NC 28202-2317
(704) 372-7170
Website: http://www.uwcentralcarolinas.org/

HOW TO ASSESS YOUR SKILLS AND TALENTS

Agencies listed at the end of this section can also help you determine which jobs suit you best by giving you an aptitude test. This test will assess your skills and talents including physical and mental aptitudes.

Your aptitude can be something you were born with, such as being physically strong, or a skill that you have learned through work experience, like building cabinets.

Aptitude usually relates to being able to do a particular skill with a good level of ability.

Achievement differs from aptitude in that achievement is a description about what you've accomplished in life. For example, owning a house can be an achievement. Completing a master's degree can be considered another achievement.

Aptitude tests assess skills, abilities, and general intelligence, whereas achievement tests reveal your knowledge and experience. Career aptitude tests inventory your job-related capabilities.

Free career tests can reveal whether or not you are qualified for a particular job. You should take career testing that helps you identify which jobs and duties you prefer.

Knowing your personality strengths is as important as testing for aptitude, achievement, or career preferences and will help determine the right job for you. Your personality is joined to your working aptitude, because some jobs are suited to your temperament and some are not. You will certainly know when a job "isn't your style," because it will not feel right. For example, if you have an analytical mind, you might prefer jobs in research, accounting, or science. An analytical person would be less likely to like repetitive work such as working on an assembly line. If you have an outgoing personality, you probably prefer managing groups of people or speaking in front of audiences.

Certain personalities fit better in certain occupations and worse in others, because different jobs demand different types of people.

Free aptitude and career testing can be found online:

www.Jobdiagnosis.com

www.ipersonic.com/career

jobsearch.about.com/od/careertests/Career_Tests.htm or the-free-career-test.com/

COMMON TERMS AND DEFINITIONS

You will find many of these terms in job ads.

Agency: An office engaged in doing business for someone else.

Applicant: A person who applies for a job.

Application: An information sheet to be filled out by a person who wants a job.

Career: The kind of work a person does for a number of years or as a specialized field.

Classified advertising: Want ads arranged according to job categories.

Dependability: A characteristic of a worker who is proven to be trusted to do what is expected.

Employment agency: An office that matches workers with jobs.

Fringe benefits: These include insurance, health benefits, pension, 401(k) plan, bonuses, paid vacation, paid days, and holidays.

Initiative: Readiness and ability to work without waiting to be told.

Cover letter: A letter written to an employer giving information about the applicant and asking for an interview.

On-the-job training (apprenticeship): Learning a skill or trade by studying and working on the job.

Pension: Regular payments received from an employer after retirement.

Qualifications: The abilities, knowledge, skills, and experience to do a job.

Recommendation: A written letter or spoken recommendation outlining a worker's qualifications and performance at a previous job.

Reference: A person who can be contacted for information about an applicant's character and abilities.

Resume: A listing of a job applicant's contact information, previous employment experience, education, skills, and references.

Want ads: Published items in the newspaper or on the Internet that describe available jobs.

WHERE TO SEARCH FOR JOBS

You must set realistic but ambitious goals. Start your search by getting a copy of your local newspaper, go to the classifieds, and look in the job section. The local newspaper is a great place to get up-to-date information on available job listings. The ads are short and to the point. Use the contact information to apply for the job.

You can access current information on the Internet at all hours of the day. It's there when you are ready to use it, even at midnight after finally getting the kids to bed.

You can reach deeper into your local area to find smaller employers closer to home, maybe even within walking distance from your house.

You can also take your search far beyond your regular boundaries. There are no geographic limits. You could choose to take a job outside your county or state.

Using the Internet in your job search will demonstrate that you have current technology skills. It tells the employer that you know how to use a computer and know how to navigate online.

Online, you can meet new people in your profession or region with much less stress. On the Internet, no one can see you sweat. Take your time getting to know people or groups before putting your best "electronic face" forward. You can explore career options that you might not have considered. What are you doing now, and are there ways to apply your skills in a new direction? You can find self-assessment tools, loads of occupations and disciplines to explore, and even lists of local career counselors and career centers to help you.

You can find jobs by visiting one of your local career help centers and by going to career fairs. [4]

"Most of the important things in the world have been accomplished by people who have kept on trying when there seemed to be no hope at all."

– *Dale Carnegie*

WANT AD ABBREVIATIONS

To reduce the cost of placing online and print classified ads, abbreviations are commonly used. Listed below are some examples of acceptable abbreviations.

Acctg	Accounting
Advc	Advancement
Aft	After
Agcy	Agency
Appt	Appointment
Avail	Available
Begnr	Beginner
Bkkppg	Bookkeeping
Btwn	Between
Bus	Bus person
Clk	Clerk
Coll Grad	College Graduate
Comm	Commission
Dept	Department
Dep	Dependable
Dict	Dictation
EOE	Equal Opportunity Employer
Equiv	Equivalent
Eves	Evenings

Exc/Excl	Excellent
Exper/Exp	Experience
Exp nec	Experience necessary
Exp per	Experience preferred
F/C	Full charge
F/Pd	Fee paid
Fcty	Factory
Gd	Good
Grad	Graduate
Hrly	Hourly
Hr	Hour
HS	High school
Immed	Immediate
Info	Information
Inq	Inquire
Intrstg	Interesting
Intvw	Interview
Jr	Junior
Loc	Location
Mfg	Manufacturing
Mgmt	Management
Mgr	Manager
Mo/M	Month
Nec	Necessary
Ovtm	Overtime
Ofc	Office
PDVAC	Paid Vacation
Perm	Permanent
P.T.	Part Time
Pref	Preferred
Req'd	Required
Rep	Representative
Reas	Reasonable

Respon	Responsible
Sal	Salary
Secty	Secretary
Sm.	Some
St	Start
Stat	Statistician
Sr	Senior
Vac	Vacation
Vet	Veteran
Vic	Vicinity
Wk	Week
W/	With
W/wo	With or without
Wkday	Weekday
Wkend	Weekend
WPM	Words per minute
Yr	Year

OTHER JOB HUNTING STRATEGIES

Temporary employment agencies. Temporary employment means that a job has a term limit (three months, six months, or longer). Using a temporary employment agency has become an increasingly popular approach to finding a job, because these jobs sometimes become permanent.

Volunteering and part time. There are many people who start as volunteer or part-time workers and become permanently employed by the company. This type of work can help you build valuable experience that you can include on your resume. It also lets a potential employer know that you want to work and are serious about finding a job. It shows that you have passion and want to keep your skills sharp, and it shows what you did between jobs. This will work to your advantage. Some volunteer sites include www.volunteermatch.com, www.sonnetwork.org, and www.serve.gov.

"The tragedy of life doesn't lie in not reaching your goal. The tragedy lies in having no goals to reach."

– *Benjamin Mays*

JOB INTERVIEW TIPS

When you get that call for a job interview, follow the advice here so that you can be at your best.

- Ask if you should arrive early to fill out an applications or paperwork before the actual interview begins. Arrive at least ten minutes before the interview.

- Dress to make the right impression by wearing a conservative outfit. Do not wear flashy clothing or jewelry.

- Make sure that you know how to get to the building and how long it takes to get there. Ask someone for a ride, or check the bus schedule if you don't have a car. Go to MapQuest.com and, if you're prone to getting lost, do a test run to the interview site the day before. Plan ahead.

- Bring along a printed copy of your resume, references, and work samples (manuals, spreadsheets, photos, etc.). Whether the interviewer wants the material or not, bringing it shows that you thought ahead and came prepared.

- As you walk in, smile, relax, breathe, and be confident. Make eye contact, introduce yourself in a pleasant tone of voice, and give a firm handshake.

- During the interview, sit up straight, show your enthusiasm, and answer all the questions as thoroughly and honestly as possible. If you don't know how to do something that the job requires, admit this and say that you want to learn.

- Think about the questions an interviewer might ask you and how you'll answer them.

Be prepared if you really want the job. Whether you are new to the workforce or switching jobs after many years, it's a good idea to brush up on your job interview skills.

"It is often said that you never get a second chance to make a good first impression."

THE FIRST IMPRESSION

Interviewers can usually tell whether or not you are the right candidate for the job within the first few minutes. The "first impression" refers to your appearance, outfit, facial expressions, and body language, and this impression can make or break it for applicants. To make a good first impression, begin by doing your homework. You applied for that job for a reason, so be sure to leave your interviewer with no doubt in her mind as to why you want it.

Obtain all the information you can about the job description, such as salary and benefits. The company's human resources department can often help you, so don't be afraid to call or send an email.

Go online or to your local library and read about the company, its history, what it makes, or who owns it. This might sound like a lot of research for an interview, but it's worth it. Your preparation lets the interviewer know that you have a high level of interest in the position.

Being educated and prepared will not only keep you calm and confident during the interview but may make the difference in landing the job.

COMMON INTERVIEW QUESTIONS AND SUGGESTED ANSWERS

Some companies have specific interview questions for job candidates. Here is a sample of list of questions that are commonly asked.

Tell me a little about yourself.
This is a common first question, and it helps to break the ice. Be careful not to give the interviewer your life story; don't try to explain everything from your birth to the present day. Give just the relevant facts about your education, career, and current life situation. Write down a few sentences in advance that sum up what you want to tell the interviewer.

Why are you looking?
This should be a straightforward question to answer, but it can trip you up. Presumably you are looking for a new job because you want to get a position that allows you to make a living. It's not a good idea to mention money, which can make you sound greedy. If you were fired, you'll need a good explanation, but stay positive. You could say, "I just got out of jail, and my parole officer said I had to get a job!"

Tell me what you know about this company.
Whether you are applying for a job as the VP of Marketing or as the mailroom clerk, know something about that company.

Who owns the company?

What is name of the person who will interview you or make the decision to hire you?

How many employees does the company have?

What kind of products or services does the company provide?

Does it have offices in the United States or other parts of the world?

What relevant experience do you have?
Be ready to explain the work, skills, training, and talents that make you right for the job. The interviewer should already have read your resume, but don't hesitate to repeat your strengths that relate to the job.

Have you done anything to further your experience?
Your answer could include anything from night classes and online research to hobbies and sports and reading magazines, newspapers, or books. If you have talked to a mentor or have a friend who has a similar job, it is worth mentioning. Anything to do with further education is great, so you can tell the interviewer about a home-improvement project that is helping you learn skills such as time management or carpentry.

Where else have you applied?
There could be two scenarios here:

1) This is your first interview. You've recently started looking for work and were happy to find a job opening that seems perfect for you.

2) You've interviewed at other companies. This tells the interviewer that though you've been looking at other jobs, this one interests you the most. This is a good way to hint that you're in demand without sounding like you're interviewing all over town. Be honest, and mention a few other companies, but don't go into detail. The fact that you're seriously looking and keeping your options open is what the interviewer is driving at.

How do you handle pressure?
There are a few ways to answer this question, but they should all be positive. You can say that you "work well" under pressure, you "thrive" under pressure, or you "prefer" working under pressure. Saying that you handle pressure "okay" or that "it's no problem" doesn't say enough to help you get your foot in the door. Think of a time when you successfully handled a lot of pressure in a previous job, and describe that.

What motivates you to do a good job?
The answer to this question is not money, even if that is the truth. Mention that you want recognition for a job well done. Also say that you want to become better at your job, or you want to help your department and company do well and be successful.

What's your greatest strength?
This is your chance to shine. You're being asked to explain why you are a great employee. You could be someone who is a great motivator, is an amazing problem solver, or has strong attention to detail. Perhaps having a lot of energy or physical strength makes you the best person for the job.

What's your biggest weakness?
Everyone has a weakness of some kind. This is a tough question, so think about it before the interview, as it usually is asked. Don't say something like "I'm too committed to my work and don't spend enough time with my family." I've heard people say, "I think I'm too good at my job, and it can often make people jealous." Provide a work-related flaw that you're working hard to improve. For example, you might say, "I've been told that I occasionally focus on details and miss the bigger picture, so I've been spending time laying out the complete project every day to see my overall progress." [5]

Some people may assume it's easy to "talk" their way through any question, handling it as it comes, but it's not so simple during an interview. Practice answering the above questions out loud.

Do your answers come out the way they should in an actual interview? If not, keep practicing, and do a little soul-searching. Be honest with yourself about your weaker skills or education, but be ready to express interest in further education and training to become a better member of the team.

When considering how to respond in an interview, think in terms of the job and the company, not about your personal life. Interviewers don't want to hear about a plan for "being married in five years" or success in "dealing with a meddling mother-in-law." They want answers specific to working experience.

Keep your answers brief (less than a minute). It helps to write down your responses and practice answering them by yourself or with a friend.

Be careful that your answers don't sound recited. Take a moment to consider the question, and collect your thoughts before answering.

Interviewees often trap themselves by answering an interview question with a negative response. For example, a question like "Why did you leave your old company?" can turn into a five-minute rant about the horrible way a former boss treated you, gossiping coworkers, or inadequate pay for the work required.

Even if that boss was a jerk, the interviewer will not be impressed by your bad-mouthing others.

To answer the question as to why you left, use common sense. Never show anger about a former boss, coworker, or company. Instead, focus on the lessons you learned from that experience.

If the interviewer asks about a skill that you don't have, never reply with, "No, I don't know how to do that" or "I've never had to do that before." Spin a potential negative answer into something positive. If you don't have a certain skill, it's appropriate to say,"I'm willing to take a night class or stay after work to learn."

When asked, "Why should we hire you?" don't rattle off all of your personal and professional achievements. Instead, relate those accomplishments to how they will contribute to bettering the company.

THANK THE INTERVIEWER

After the interview, send a thank-you letter and mention again how interested you are in the position. This is a courteous way of letting the company know that you appreciate the opportunity to interview for the job. Showing gratitude can definitely pay off. A simple gesture like this can often help you beat out applicants who are just as or even more qualified.

Write and mail a thank-you note the same day of the interview. Your note may be typed or handwritten if you have good penmanship.

Use the same paper you used for your resume, and mail it in a matching envelope. You may use a card with the words "Thank You" imprinted on the front. The font and/or type should be simple, professional, and elegant. A note card that bears a small, graphic design (such as a narrow, colored border stripe) is acceptable.

Avoid using note cards or paper that have a decorative picture, a do not use scented or fragrance paper.

Date the note in full (for example, August 15, 2020, not 08/15/20.) Greet the interviewer with "Dear Mr. Jones" or "Dear Ms. Jones."

Write your message. Be direct and personable without being personal. Use good grammar. Your message should not be longer than two short paragraphs.

Begin by giving recognition to the interviewer and the company. For example: "It was my pleasure to meet with you this afternoon regarding the auto mechanic position with Crown Ford. Thank you for the brief history of Crown Ford and for providing me with a glimpse at the company's future growth plans. They are both quite impressive."

Give recognition to yourself. Mention something from the interview that will prompt the interviewer to remember you individually. For example: "I came away from our interview with a strong sense that my qualifications and experience are an excellent match to the auto mechanic position. I believe that by sharing my skills and ideas with your talented team, and while gaining the knowledge and plans of my colleagues, we will achieve the goals you've described. I anticipate speaking with you again soon."

Offer some new information or additional reasons that the employer will be interested in you.

Close your message with "Respectfully" or "Sincerely."

If your note has been typed, type your name, and sign it in black or blue ink.

Address the envelope with the full name and title of the interviewer on the first line (Mr. Charles F. Clinton, Manager of the Service Department). The second line of the address is the company name (Crown Ford), and the third and fourth lines are for the full mailing address and ZIP code. Include your name and address in the return address area of the envelope, not on the back. [6]

NEGOTIATING A SALARY

Don't walk into an interview expecting or demanding double the figure being offered. Familiarize yourself with the rules for negotiating this often touchy subject.

Find out how much people in your field are currently making. Researching online at salary.com is simple, and remember that geography plays a role in salaries. The cost of living can vary widely from city to city and state to state.

Have a flexible salary range in mind from the minimum figure to the figure that may be a "long shot." What you currently make doesn't always have a bearing on the job in question.

An interviewer will assume that each applicant is looking for a higher salary. When applicants have the right background, professionalism, and qualifications, they should ask for what they're worth!

Never bring up the subject of money until the interviewer does. Once the topic is on the table, give a range and mention that the salary is one factor in the total compensation package that you're concerned with.

Avoid bringing up salary at the end of the interview when asked if you have any more questions. End the interview by asking for clarification or expected next steps.

Thank the interviewer for his time and offer to follow up with him in a few days.

Send a thank-you note that reiterates your interest in the position.

Now, go find a job! Don't let anyone tell convince you that jobs are not there because we are in a "down economy." The economy is always in flux, so be prepared to showcase your best skills.

That opportunity will come, just be ready!

"Opportunity is missed by most people, because it is dressed in overalls and looks like work."

– *Thomas Edison*

TIPS FOR KEEPING THE JOB

When you get a job, the employer's basic expectations include the following.

- Come to work every day, on time and dressed appropriately.

- Listen carefully to all instructions, and make sure that you understand them. Ask questions if you don't.

- Perform at your best skill level at all times, and broaden your skills so that you can stay competitive.

- Never leave work without letting your supervisor know where you are going and why you are going there. Learn to manage your emotions, and do your best to get along with coworkers. A negative attitude, being disrespectful, or having an annoying personality may cause you to lose the job.

- Manage your time well, and work as efficiently as possible.

- Take only the breaks you are allowed. Don't do your personal business on the job, and never discuss your criminal past with coworkers. The company managers hired you, so they already know your past history and are the only ones who need to know.Don't borrow or take anything from the job without written permission.

- If you are going to be late or absent, call in as soon as possible. The company may need to adjust the schedules and temporarily replace you with someone else.

- Away from the job, exercising, meditation, and other activities that reduce stress will keep you energized, focused, and relaxed.

- Surround yourself with positive people who work to improve their lives and move forward.

"Your attitude, not your aptitude, determines your altitude."
– *Zig Ziglar*

WHAT IS MY TAKE HOME PAY?

There is a difference between your gross salary and your net salary (your "take home pay"). Let us start by calculating your gross salary.

Say that you work 8 hours a day, 5 days a week (8 x 5), which equals 40 hours. Your rate of pay is $10 per hour. Your net salary is the amount left after your employer takes out federal and state taxes, your cost for a medical plan, Social Security taxes, and other deductions.

Paying Taxes

All citizens earning an income must pay taxes on that income. This money is used to pay for essential services in your city; the police, firemen, and all the other services that the city needs to operate and fulfill the needs of its citizens. State and federal taxes are used in the same way. Social Security and Medicare ensure that all working citizens have some supplementary income and medical care when they are senior citizens and retired.

Taxes are deducted before you receive your check, which will usually have a statement attached explaining the deductions. How much will your deductions be?

Federal tax on $400 a week is 25 percent or $100. Your state tax is 7.75 percent or $31. Social Security (or FICA) is 6.2 percent or approximately $22. Medicare is 1.45 percent or about $7.50. Let's add these deductions: $100 + $31 + $22

+ $7.50 = $160.50. **Your net (take home) pay is $400 – $160.50 or $239.50.**

Budgeting Your Salary

Now that you have an income, you need to learn how to budget. Budgeting is allocating a sum of money for a particular purpose.

Say that you share an apartment with a friend, and the monthly rent is $450. You are responsible for half of the rent ($225) and the entire cable bill, which is $70. This totals to $520 per month, and your portion is half of that or $260 per month (about $58 a week). Your other necessities like food, transportation, entertainment, and other miscellaneous expenses come to $125 a week. Add $125 to $58. This equals **$183 per week,** so you have **$56.50 after weekly expenses.**

Weekly income: $239.50 (net)
Weekly expenses: $183.00
Weekly amount left over: $56.50

"Do you know what happens when you give a procrastinator a good idea? Nothing!"

– *Donald Gardner*

START SAVINGS AND CHECKING ACCOUNTS

Visit your local bank and have the representative explain the different types of checking and savings accounts. Open accounts that are tailored to your needs (free checking, direct deposit, overdraft protection, etc.). Each week, put your portion of the rent, phone, and cable bill into your checking account and twenty-five dollars in your savings account. Savings can be used for a specific goal, or it can be used in case of an emergency. It is vitally important to have these accounts if you want stay out of financial trouble.

Know that the interest rates for savings accounts are typically low.

Getting a credit card

Go to different banks and shop for a credit card that fits your needs. Look for ones with the lowest interest rate and lowest late payment fees. Having a credit card will benefit you in many ways. It will help you establish a good credit rating, which you will need when you want to make a large purchase on credit like a house or a car. It can also be useful in case of an emergency when you do not have the funds available.

BANKING TERMS

Account balance history

A snapshot of your available balance, which reflects holds and transactions that are processing or cleared. This balance is used in making payment decisions and in triggering returned items or overdraft fees.

Account statement

A printed or online statement of all debit and credit transactions on an account for a given statement cycle.

Active account

A bank account in which there are recent transactions.

Annual percentage yield (APY)

A percentage rate reflecting the total amount of interest paid on a deposit account (checking, savings, CDs, IRAs), based on the interest rate and the effect of interest compounding for one year.

Automatic funds transfer

An arrangement that moves funds from one account to another automatically on a prearranged schedule (for example, every payday or once a month).

Automatic payment

An arrangement that authorizes payments to be deducted

automatically from a bank account (usually a checking account) to pay bills such as insurance payments, rent, mortgage or loan payments. Payments are usually scheduled for a certain day of the month.

Available balance

Your available balance is the amount of money in your checking or savings account that is currently available for you. It includes all cleared and processing transactions. Keep in mind that any transactions you have made but your bank has not yet received need to be subtracted from your available balance to know the exact amount of money you have to spend or withdraw.

Average daily balance

Balances during an accounting period, usually a monthly statement cycle, divided by the number of days in the period. Can sometimes be used to calculate whether a service charge applies or to qualify for special services.

Banking center

A bank's branch office. Banks usually have many banking centers in your city or state. Large banks have banking centers throughout the country.

Bill pay

Bill pay is an optional service from some banks that allows you to pay your bills online. In addition, you can elect to receive e-bills (electronic versions of your paper bills) from your bank or from a company.

Bounced check

A check that a bank returns unpaid because there are not enough available funds in the account.

Cancelled check

A check that has been paid. A cancelled check may generally be used as proof of payment.

Cashier's check

A check drawn on and issued by a bank. It does not usually bounce, because its amount is paid to the bank when it is issued, and the bank then assumes the obligation.

Certificate of Deposit (CD)

A time deposit that is payable at the end of a specific term. CDs generally pay a fixed interest rate and generally offer a higher interest rate than other types of deposit accounts. Terms can range from seven days to 10 years. CDs are insured by the FDIC up to the maximum allowed by law. If an early withdrawal from the CD prior to the end of the term is permitted, a penalty is usually assessed.

Certified check

A check for which the bank guarantees payment.

Checking account

A type of deposit account, sometimes interest bearing, which enables customers to place funds and withdraw the available funds on demand, typically by writing a check.

Debit

A financial term that refers to a decrease in a deposit account balance, such as a check posted to the account.

Debit card

A plastic card issued by a bank that customers can use anywhere Visa card or MasterCard is accepted. Because money is deducted directly from a designated checking account, there are no interest charges. A debit card can also be used at an ATM, so there is no need to carry both a debit card and an ATM card (also referred to as a debit card).

Deposit

Money added into a customer's account at a financial institution.

Direct deposit

With direct deposit, deposits are made electronically into your checking, savings, or money market account. Deposits can include salary, pension, Social Security and Supplemental Security Income (SSI) benefits, or other regular sources of income.

Disclosure

Information pertaining to the account services and regulatory requirements.

Electronic Funds Transfer (EFT)

A transfer of funds initiated by electronic means such as an electronic terminal, telephone, computer, ATM, or magnetic tape.

FDIC

The Federal Deposit Insurance Corporation (FDIC) is an independent agency of the U.S. government. The FDIC protects depositors against the loss of their insured deposits if a bank or savings associate fails. FDIC insurance is back by the full faith and credit of the United States government.

The FDIC guarantees deposit accounts (checking, savings, money market savings, and CDs) up to the maximum allowed by law. In October 2008, the FDIC temporarily increased basic deposit insurance from $100,000 to $250,000 per depositor through December 31, 2013. The FDIC separately guarantees individual retirement accounts (IRAs) up to $250,000 per owner.

Hold

Deposit holds are delays to the availability of a portion of a deposited check. They occur infrequently, and it you receive one; you will receive a notice with the reason and the date that the funds will be available. The date on the hold notice will replace the "Credit Pending" date for that portion of the deposit.

Balance holds are holds placed on your entire account balance.

Inactive account

A bank account in which there have been no transactions for an extended period of time. In some cases (such as no activity within the period specified by state law, generally at least three years), the law requires the bank to turn the account over to the state as unclaimed property.

Interest bearing

An account that earns interest is an "interest-bearing account."

Interest rate

The rate paid on an interest-bearing account such as savings, CDs, and some checking accounts. The rates paid or charged on loans can differ.

Maturity date

The date when the term of your CD ends. Withdrawals before maturity are usually subject to a substantial penalty.

Minimum daily balance

The lowest end-of-day balance in an account during a statement cycle. It is often required to be kept in an account each day to earn interest, to avoid a service charge, or to qualify for special service.

Money market account

A savings account that generally permits up to three withdrawals by check or debit card each statement cycle.

Money order

A financial instrument, issued by a bank or other institution, allowing the person named on the order to receive a specified amount of cash on demand. Often used by people who don't have checking accounts.

Monthly maintenance fee

The fee charged to main a particular account such as a checking account.

Online banking

A service that allows an account holder to obtain account information and manage certain banking transactions, including bill payment, by computer.

Original interest rate

The rate assigned when a Certificate of Deposit account is opened.

Overdraft

An overdraft occurs when you do not have enough available funds in your account to cover a check or other withdrawal; the bank pays the items and overdraws your account.

Overdraft protection

A service that allows a checking account to be linked to another account that provides protection against returned items or overdrafts. When your checking account does not have sufficient funds to cover a check, funds are automatically transferred from the available balance in the linked account.

Personal identification number (PIN)

A Personal Identification Number (PIN) is the number that customers use with their ATM or debit card to access their accounts at ATMs or to make purchases with their debit card. The number should always be kept confidential.

Simple interest

The interest calculated on a principal sum, not compounded on earned interest.

Stop payment

When you ask a bank not to pay a check or payment you have written or authorized. Stop payments are generally placed on lost or stolen checks or on checks related to disputed purchases. Stop payment orders generally expire after six months, and a fee usually applies.

Time deposit or CD

An account for a fixed term with the understanding that the funds will remain on deposit until the end of the term. Penalties for early withdrawals may apply.

Transaction limitations

Refers to a Federal Reserve Board regulation that limits certain types of withdrawals and/or transfers from savings and money market deposit accounts. There can be no more than six preauthorized or automatic transfers or telephone/PC transfers out of the account each month. Of the six, if applicable, no more than three of the six limited transfers may be check or debit card. Withdrawals at ATMs and teller windows from these accounts are unlimited.

Transfer

A movement of funds from one account to another.

Travelers check

A check issued by a financial institution that functions like cash but is protected against loss or theft. These checks are useful when traveling.

Variable rate

An interest rate that may fluctuate during the term of a loan, line of credit, or deposit account. Sometimes the rate changes based on changes in an index rate such as the prime rate or other prescribed criteria. The bank may change the rate at its discretion.

Withdrawal

Removal of funds from an account.

Zero Liability Protection

A bank's guarantee. If your card is lost or stolen, you may not be responsible for unauthorized purchases made with your card if you report the theft promptly. The Zero Liability Protection program is free and automatically available on many consumer credit cards. [7]

CONCLUSION

After listening to today's news media, you may get the impression that there are no jobs available, but thousands of people still find jobs. In addition to believing in yourself, believing that it's going to happen and thinking positive, you will still be required to do some work. "Working my way back" explains in plain simple language what needs to be done.

This book is a guide that when used correctly, will help you to get and keep a well-paying job in your field. You may have to review it more than once to be sure you have understood and followed all the instructions.

While writing this book, I thought of my own meager beginnings. I am the product of the "Jim Crow" south, a sharecropper's son. At age twelve, my family moved to Philadelphia, PA in search of jobs and a better way of life. While there, I got into trouble with the law (misdemeanor stuff) and went to reform school. I always believed that education was the pathway out of poverty. So I went to school and received a bachelor's degree and two master's degrees. I taught high school in the New York school system for twenty five years and served as an administrator for four and a half years. I am now retired. If you follow the instructions, you will have a chance at a similar fulfilling experience.

REFERENCES

1. Goodwill Industries International, 15810 Indianola Drive Rockville, MD 20855 (800) 741-0186.

2. http://www.michigan.gov/documents/CoverLetter_13348_7.pdf.

3. Boston College, The Trustees of Boston College.

4. Margaret F. Dikel, The Riley Guide- 11218 Ashley Dr. Rockville, MD 20852 (240)-602-6043 http://www.rileyguide.com/jobsrch.hml

5. Paul Michael, http://www.wisebread.com/how-to-answer-23-of- the-most-common interview-questions 4 October 2007

6. http://www.wikihow.com/Write-an-Interview-Thank-You-Note.

7. Bank of America, P.O. Box 25118 Tampa Fl. 33622-5118 (800) 432-1000 http://www.bankofamerica.com/deposit/checksave/index .cfm?template=lcglossary

CPSIA information can be obtained
at www.ICGtesting.com
Printed in the USA
LVOW10s1442110817
544663LV00011B/444/P